PLANTS

lady's slipper orchid

NATIONAL GEOGRAPHIC NATURE LIBRARY

PLANTS

NATIONAL GEOGRAPHIC NATURE LIBRARY

by Catherine Herbert Howell

NATIONAL GEOGRAPHIC SOCIETY

Washington, D.C.

*All photographs supplied by the
Earth Scenes Division of
Animals Animals Enterprises*

daffodils

Table of Contents

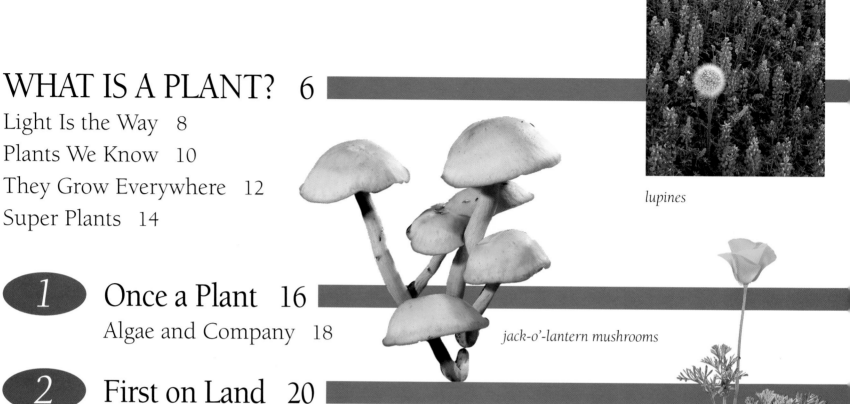

lupines

jack-o'-lantern mushrooms

California poppy

dwarf irises

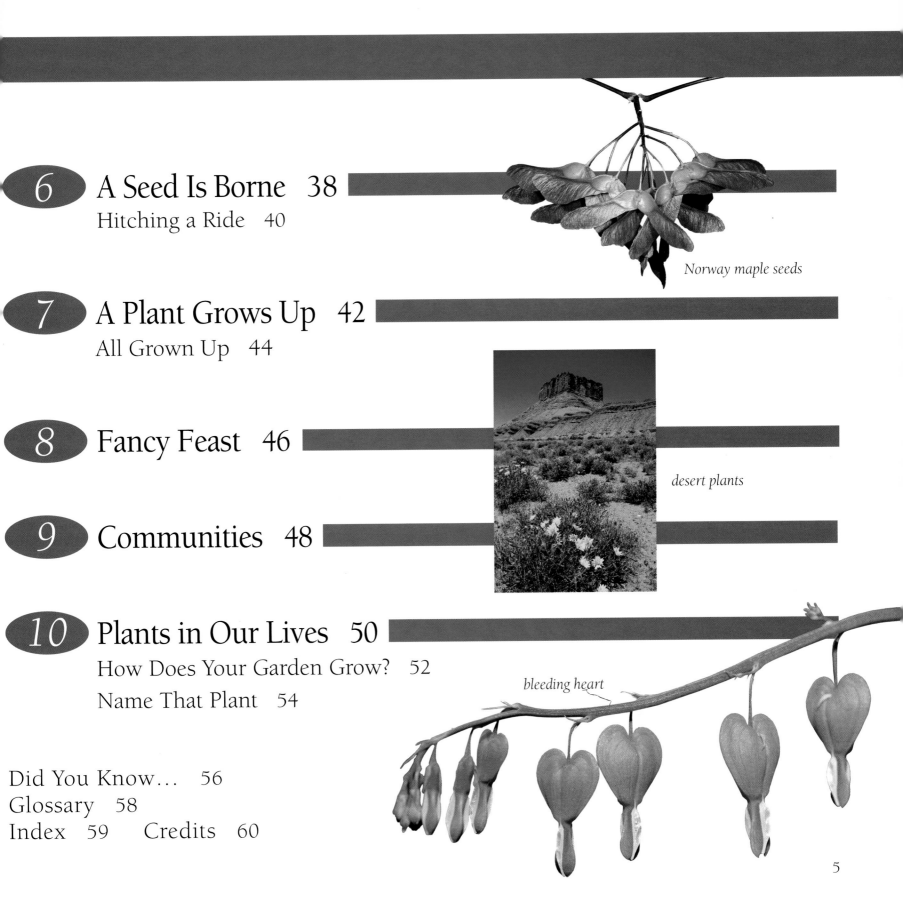

WHAT IS A PLANT?

Plants are living things with a very special ability. They take the energy of the sun's light and change it into food for themselves. There are about 300,000 species, or kinds, of plants in the world. A delicate orchid and a sturdy tulip poplar tree are both plants, living in the same ways and having the same needs as other plants.

- Most plants MAKE THEIR OWN FOOD, using sunlight, water, and air in a PROCESS CALLED PHOTOSYNTHESIS (foe-toe-SIN-thuh-sis).

- As part of photosynthesis, plants MAKE most of earth's OXYGEN.

- Plants continue to GROW THROUGHOUT THEIR LIVES, sometimes very slowly.

- Most plants HAVE ROOTS, STEMS, LEAVES, and FLOWERS.

- Most plants REPRODUCE BY MEANS OF SEEDS OR SPORES.

- Most plants are at least partly GREEN.

- Plants PROVIDE ENERGY for people and other animals.

passionflower vine

blue spruce

horsetail

pickerelweed

tulip poplar

lady's slipper
orchid

fern

blueberries

moss

red cabbage

prickly pear cactus

7

Light Is the Way

Like many living things, including humans, plants need light to grow and thrive. Plants, though, also need light for basic survival. Light energy is the ingredient that starts the process of photosynthesis— the way most green plants make their own food. In addition to water and soil containing minerals, plants need light to grow. Sunlight is nature's way, but artificial light can also power the process of photosynthesis.

LIGHT FROM THE LEAF

To make food—or photosynthesize— a plant such as this pumpkin vine must take in water from the ground through its roots. The water travels up the stem to the leaves. The leaves themselves take in carbon dioxide, a gas, from the air. Photosynthesis occurs when sunlight strikes tiny particles called chlorophyll (KLORE-uh-fill) that give leaves their green color. Chlorophyll changes the water and carbon dioxide into a sugary food called glucose. Glucose travels to different parts of the plant and provides energy for growth. The chemical changes that occur in photosynthesis create "leftover" oxygen.

Sunlight is necessary for photosynthesis.

Oxygen created in photosynthesis exits through the leaves.

Leaves take in carbon dioxide.

Roots take in water as well as nutrients such as nitrogen and potassium that plants need for growth.

A plant feeds itself a meal of high-energy sugars, called glucose, that it made in its own leaves

LIGHT SHOW

Since plants can't move from place to place, they have their food delivered. In a forest, light strikes the upper branches of tall trees first and starts the food-making process. Shorter trees and plants receive less light. If it's not enough, they won't survive.

9

Plants We Know

When you were a baby, one of the first things you may have noticed—after your family and pets—was probably a plant. A bright red tulip, shimmering green grass, cheery yellow daffodils, and colorful autumn trees easily grab attention. These are plants familiar to us.

ALL FOR FALL
In the fall, the leaves of some trees turn from green to red, gold, or orange, then drop from their branches. Reduced light and cooler weather cause this change.

FLOWER POWER
Bright blue lupines bloom in a field. Some lupines can grow to five feet tall. Lupine nectar is a favorite food of butterflies.

We eat the barley plant's seeds, known as grains, usually in breads and cereals.

GREAT GRAINS
What do you have in common with a cow? You both eat grass, although in different forms. The barley shown here—along with wheat, oats, and rice—is one of many grasses people often eat.

Magnolias may grow to heights of up to 80 feet.

MAGNIFICENT MAGNOLIA

You might not think of a tree as a flowering plant, but many are. The broad trunk of this magnolia is actually a stem. The stem supports branches with leaves, flowers, and fuzzy red fruit that contains seeds.

Magnolias are among earth's oldest flowering plants.

11

They Grow Everywhere

Plants don't ask for much. Given their basic needs—light, water, and minerals—plants can survive almost anywhere. They can live in the ground, in the water, and even in the air. Plants have adapted, or adjusted, to life all over the world, from high, cold mountains to scorching deserts.

As any home gardener knows, dandelions are tough plants.

JUST DANDY
A sidewalk crack provides just enough space for this dandelion to grow. The dandelion sends a long root into the soil under the pavement.

SNOW PROBLEM
The delicate flowers of the snowbell poke above frosty snow on a mountain slope in the Alps. Flowers get an early start on growth in the mountains because warm weather there lasts only a short time. Mountain flowers begin to grow when they feel the warmth of the sun—even before the snow melts.

LIVING ON AIR
Air plants hang from the limb of a mangrove tree. Air plants use some roots to grab the limb. The rest of the roots dangle in the air and absorb moisture from it.

LOST IN SPACE
Fuzzy lava cactuses cling to moon-like folds of hardened lava in the Galápagos Islands. Shallow roots let the cactus grow in small cracks in the rock. Cactuses have adapted to the dry Galápagos and other desert climates by storing water in their fleshy stems.

MORE THAN MEETS THE EYE
Graceful water lilies float on a pond's surface. The lilies look like they're on their own, but long, strong stems hold the leaves and flowers up. Roots anchor the plants in the pond's muddy bottom.

Super Plants

Some plants are among the smallest living things on earth; others are the tallest, the widest, or the heaviest. Some individual plants have survived for thousands of years and are among the oldest things in the world. Plant parts are equally awesome. Flowers, for example, range from the tiny blossoms of the duckweed to the yard-wide blooms of the rafflesia (ruh-FLEE-zhuh) of southeastern Asia.

OLD GLORY
Weathered by centuries in the sun, this bristlecone pine was growing in the California desert when the pyramids were rising in Egypt. The oldest known bristlecone is about 4,800 years old. Bristlecones grow slowly.

Rafflesia blossoms give off an unusual smell. It attracts flies that spread the plant's pollen.

AWESOME BLOSSOMS
Red blossoms the size of hula hoops give the rafflesia first place in flower size. A flower can weigh in at 15 pounds, about as much as a bowling ball.

DINKY DUCKWEED

The tiny flower of the duckweed plant is the world's smallest, measuring only about 1/50 of an inch across. That's smaller than the head of a pin. Duckweed is a favorite food of ducks and other pond animals. It grows quickly, often covering the surface of a pond.

General Sherman stands 275 feet tall. The combination of its height and width make it the most massive living thing in the world.

RING AROUND THE GENERAL

It would take a classroom full of kids to encircle General Sherman, a giant sequoia (sih-KWOY-uh) that grows in California. Named for a Civil War leader, the tree is more than a hundred feet around at its base.

1 Once a Plant

Scientists once grouped the plant-like life-forms algae (AL-gee) and fungi (FUN-jie) with plants. Algae and fungi share some traits with plants. Algae, for example, make food through photosynthesis. Fungi reproduce the same way some plants do. But algae and fungi are different enough from plants and each other that scientists now put them in separate groups. In addition to photosynthesizing food, algae can absorb nutrients from other organisms. Fungi cannot photosynthesize. They feed on other life-forms.

Kelp, like all seaweed, is a kind of algae.

Watch out where you swim! A "swamp creature" wears the slimy green algae found in ponds and other slow-moving bodies of water.

SLIME TIME
Frothy green algae swirl around rocks at a river's edge. Some algae are made up of just one cell. Most algae live in water or in places that are very damp.

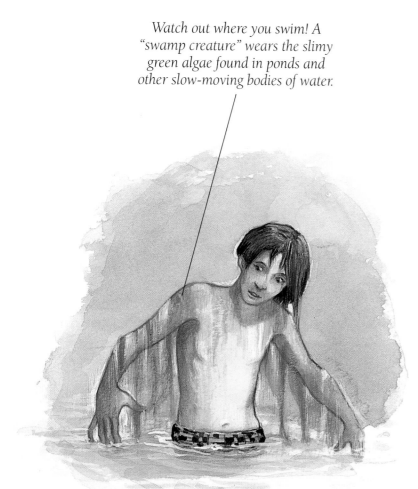

HELP FROM KELP

Sea otters frolic in giant kelp, a type of seaweed that grows in the Pacific Ocean. Otters wrap themselves in kelp to keep from drifting while they nap. A strand of kelp can reach 200 feet in length.

Egg-shaped bladders, or air bags, keep kelp afloat in the water.

PRETTY IN PINK

Snow algae tint a glacier in Antarctica. A layer of snow protects the algae in winter. In summer they grow toward the surface to receive light and a little moisture from snowmelt.

Algae and Company

Algae and fungi are very old life-forms. Algae made of single cells existed in ancient oceans more than two billion years ago. Many-celled green algae may be the ancestors of all land plants. Fungi can be single-celled, like the yeast that makes bread rise, or many-celled, like mushrooms. Fungi feed on dead or decaying organisms as well as on living matter. A lichen (LIKE-en) is a partnership between a type of fungus and a colony of algae.

This alga and this fungus took a "lichen" to each other.

FANCY FUNGUS

Mushrooms are probably the most familiar fungi. They live in damp places with plenty of decayed matter to feed on. Most fungi live on land.

These mushrooms are called jack-o'-lanterns for their orange color.

EMPTY SHELVES

Bracket fungus grows like shelves on a fallen log. The fungus feeds on the decaying wood, breaking down the wood's tough cell walls and releasing nutrients. Insects, other animals, and plants use the nutrients.

LICHEN PARTNERS ▶

Lichens color rocks along the North Sea in England. The algae in lichens make food for the organisms through photosynthesis, while the fungi absorb food and water. Two ways of feeding allow lichens to survive in places other life-forms could not—such as on rocks or in snow. Lichens help break down rock to make soil.

18

2 First on Land

The first plants that grew on land, about 430 million years ago, did not look like the plants we know. Early plants had upright stems and no roots or leaves. By the time dinosaurs roamed, plants were more familiar looking. Ferns, horsetails, and club mosses are the plants of today most closely related to ancient plants. They all produce spores to make new plants.

JUST SAY NEIGH
The stems of horsetails grow in a ringed pattern. Among the most ancient of plants, giant horsetails formed a large part of the plant life that turned into coal deposits millions of years ago.

JOIN THE CLUB
Club moss covers a log in the Hoh Rain Forest in Washington State. Club moss has roots, stems, and tiny leaves like needles.

SPORES AND MORE
A fern shows the sporangia (spah-RAN-gee-uh) on the underside of its fronds, or leaves. Spores develop inside the sporangia and are released when ripe. Each spore can sprout into a tiny plant with both male and female parts. These parts unite and form a new fern plant. Horsetails and club mosses also grow this way.

DINO DINER
A plant-eating dinosaur munches at a Jurassic "salad bar." Ferns, horsetails, cycads, and other early plants often grew to huge sizes, satisfying the appetites of the giant plant eaters, or herbivores (ER-buh-vorz).

cycad

fern

horsetail

3 Plants Take Hold

Roots help a plant get a grip on life. One job of roots is to anchor a plant so that it can grow in soil. Roots also absorb water and minerals from the soil and store nutrients made in the plant's leaves. Roots can cover a lot of space underground: A single grass plant can send its root system over hundreds of yards of soil.

Each strawberry runner is a miniature of the parent plant.

STRAWBERRY FIELDS
A strawberry plant spreads itself around by sending out runners. A runner is a long stem with a baby plant attached. The runner grows along the ground and then stops, and the new plant puts down roots.

TREE ON STILTS
The roots of a Brazilian palm tree rise above the ground. The roots are covered with tiny hairs that take in air and moisture for the tree.

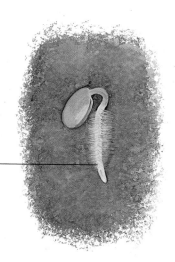

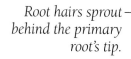

Root hairs sprout behind the primary root's tip.

THE ROOT OF THE MATTER

The root is the first part of a plant to sprout. All plants develop a primary root that starts the job of anchoring the plant and absorbing water. A plant's root system then forms in one of two ways. A plant such as a carrot sends a long, thin taproot deep down into the soil for water and nutrients. Other plants, such as grasses, grow thin fibrous roots that branch again and again from the primary root. On both kinds of roots, fine hairs—called root hairs—do the main work of absorbing water and nutrients.

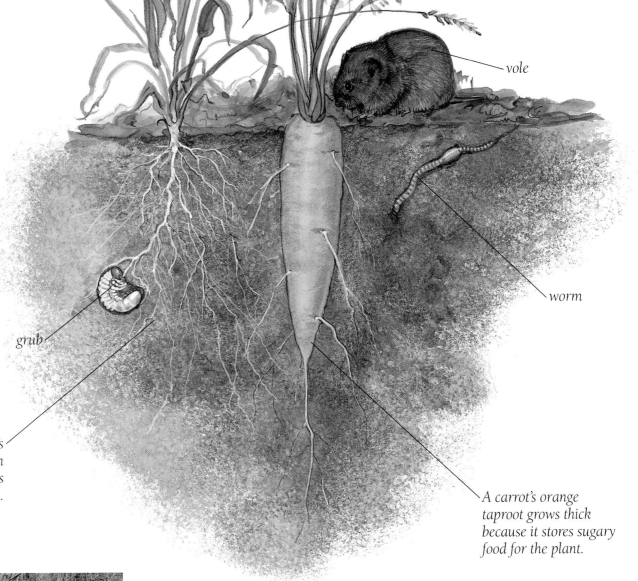

vole

worm

grub

A grass plant's fibrous root system can have billions of root hairs.

A carrot's orange taproot grows thick because it stores sugary food for the plant.

UPROOTED

A toppled tree shows the roots that once anchored it. Many trees have long tap roots that reach down to water and shorter fibrous roots to catch rain. A tree's roots usually extend in a circle underground that matches the widest spread of the leaves above.

23

Making Connections

When it comes to doing its job, a plant's stem rises to the occasion. A stem holds up the plant and provides support for all of its parts. Special tissue inside stems, called xylem (ZIE-lum), transports water and minerals absorbed by the roots. Other tissue, called phloem (FLOW-em), sends around the food made by photosynthesis.

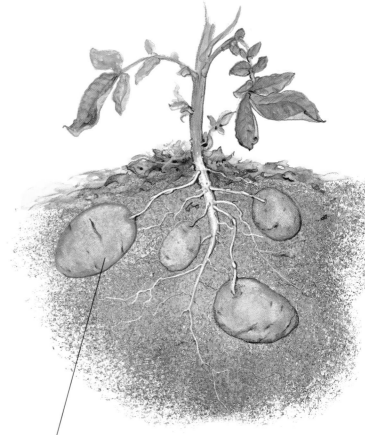

Potatoes were first used for food in South America about 6,000 years ago.

FRIES FROM DOWN UNDER
Potato plants send up stems with leaves and flowers. They send other stems, which are the part we eat, underground. The "eyes" of the potato are actually tiny new plants.

FLOATING ON AIR
Purple water lilies rise from a pond. Air-filled tubes inside the stems help hold up the blossoms and also send air from the leaves to the lilies' roots.

STICK 'EM UP

A tall central stem braces a saguaro (suh-WAHR-oh) cactus in the Arizona desert. The plant's "arms" sprout from the main stem. Saguaro stems contain chlorophyll and work as leaves do in photosynthesis. They also store water to help the plant survive the desert's dryness.

PRETTY POPPY

A golden flower crowns the California poppy. A slender stem is all that's needed to support the delicate, four-petaled blossom.

The sturdy stem of a poppy contains both xylem and phloem.

25

Green Machines

A plant's most important work is performed in the leaves. Leaves take care of the plant's survival through photosynthesis. They also produce the oxygen necessary to most other life-forms on earth. Most leaves have a flat blade that is strengthened by a network of veins. The blade grows on a stalk called a petiole (PEH-tee-ole). A petiole rotates during the day so that a leaf receives the most sunlight possible to help it photosynthesize.

NEEDLE SHARP
Pine trees and other evergreens keep their leaves in winter. Pine needles have a waxy coating that helps keep them from freezing.

Pine needles contain a kind of antifreeze.

Their long, narrow, and flat shape also helps keep pine needles from freezing.

IN DYING COLOR
The leaves of most deciduous (dih-SIH-juh-wuhs) trees change color in the fall. Green fades from the leaves as weaker light and cooler nights stop the production of chlorophyll. Other colors in the leaves then show. Photosynthesis stops. Soon the leaves dry out and begin to drop from their branches. The fallen leaves will add nutrients to the soil.

LEAF LINES

Leaves come in many shapes and sizes. Leaf shape helps to identify plants. A simple leaf has only one blade on a petiole. A compound leaf has a number of blades, or leaflets, on a single petiole.

Stinging nettles have a heart-shaped leaf with jagged edges. The leaf's bristly hairs cause painful stings.

The leaf of the tulip poplar tree is symmetrical and has four sections, or lobes.

The spaces between the leaflets of a compound leaf, such as this honey locust, allow light to reach other leaves on the plant.

Deciduous trees are adapted to losing all their leaves in the fall and growing new ones in the spring.

Evergreens lose some of their leaves—usually needles—and grow new ones all the time, so the tree is never bare.

27

4 Conifers and Cousins

Conifers get their name from the cones they bear. Conifers—among them pines, firs, and spruces—and their relatives, such as cycads, were the first plants on earth to produce seeds. These trees have seeds in cones. Each tree has both male and female cones. The male cone makes fine pollen that is blown onto a female cone and unites with an egg inside. This union produces a seed.

When the seeds of a female cone are ripe, the cone's scales loosen and spread out.

PINING AWAY
A stand of graceful Jeffrey pines covers a mountain slope in California. Pines and other conifers are often grown for their long, straight trunks that provide good lumber.

Each scale of a female pine cone usually bears two seeds.

CONE HEADS
Seed factories for conifers, female cones vary in size and shape. A one-inch redwood cone is roundish, while a 15-inch-long sugar pine cone looks narrow.

redwood

Cone size does not reflect the size of the tree. A redwood can grow to more than 350 feet.

sugar pine

LIVING FOSSIL ▶
The female cone of a prickly cycad displays a precise pattern of scales. Cycads, which look a lot like palm trees, have changed little since they first appeared on earth, some 280 million years ago.

28

5 Flowering Plants

Ⓦe admire flowers for their beauty and the pleasure they bring. For flowering plants, though, a flower is a link to the future. A flower contains all the parts the plant needs to form seeds. The seeds of flowering plants, unlike those of conifers, develop inside the flower instead of in a cone. Flowering plants appeared about 145 million years ago. Today nine out of ten plants on earth bear flowers.

DOUBLE DUTY
Each flower, such as this lily, contains both male and female parts. The male part of a flower is the stamen, and the female is the pistil. The anther, part of the stamen, produces male reproductive cells called pollen. The stigma, part of the pistil, receives the pollen. It travels to the ovary, where it fertilizes the egg inside. The fertilized egg forms seeds.

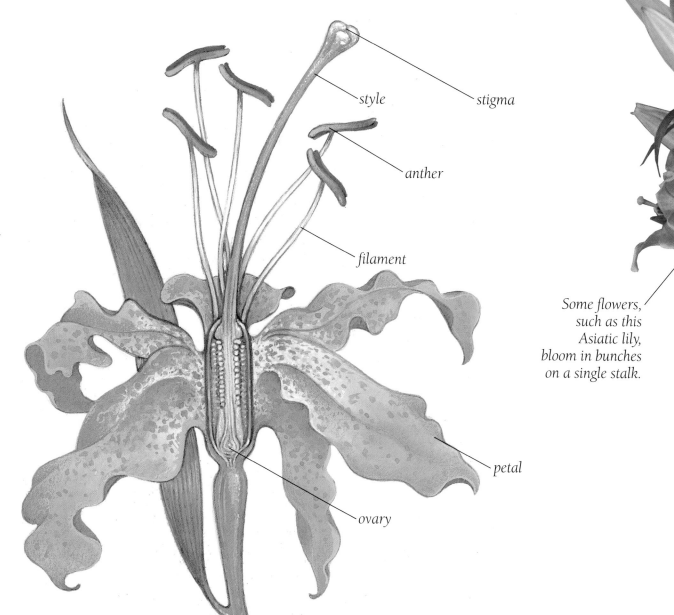

style

stigma

anther

filament

petal

ovary

Some flowers, such as this Asiatic lily, bloom in bunches on a single stalk.

30

BUNCH OF BEAUTIES
Flowering plants display an amazing range of size and appearance. Yet each flower has the same mission in life—to produce seeds.

This gerbera daisy is a kind of flower that blooms one to a stalk.

Pathways of Pollen

Pollen is the first step toward a new generation of plants. The male parts, or anthers, of flowering plants produce pollen. It must reach a flower's female part, or pistil, to fertilize the egg inside. Most eggs are not fertilized by pollen from their same plant. They must receive pollen from another plant. Wind, water, and animals carry pollen to other flowers.

STICKY FINGERS

Powdery yellow pollen from a cattail clings to fingers. Humans sometimes spread pollen when they work in their gardens. A single plant can produce millions of pollen grains.

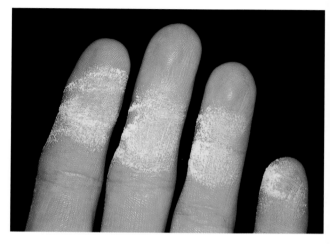

BLOWING IN THE WIND

Small clouds of pollen swirl from the tiny flowers of meadow foxtail grass. The wind can blow pollen thousands of miles before it drifts down to a flower and pollinates it.

Pollen falling into a stream often bunches together in a pollen "raft." The pollen of each plant species is unique in size, shape, and surface pattern.

POLLEN PICKUP

A honeybee prepares to land on an apple blossom. The bee's diet of pollen and nectar draws it to the flower. Pollen sticks to the bee's body as it eats, and will be deposited on another flower when the bee drops in for its next meal.

A blackberry plant shows the transformation from flower to seed-bearing fruit.

FLOWER TO FRUIT

After pollination and fertilization, a blackberry flower's petals fall off. Other parts gradually change shape, taking the form of a bumpy berry. Each bump, or drupelet (DROO-plet), contains a seed. All flowering plants make seed-filled fruit.

33

Basic Attraction

Flowering plants that are pollinated by the wind are usually small and not very showy. Those that rely on animals for pollination have special features that lure these potential pollinators. A plant's color, smell, or pattern will lead the animals to the flower's yummy nectar and pollen.

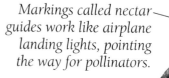

Markings called nectar guides work like airplane landing lights, pointing the way for pollinators.

RAINBOW CONNECTION

A rainbow lorikeet feasts on the nectar of callistemon flowers in Australia. Birds, which lack a strong sense of smell, are attracted by red and orange flowers.

YOU'RE THE ONE

Only a certain kind of hawkmoth has a mouthpart long enough to reach the narrow nectar tubes of the Madagascar moth orchid. This moth is the orchid's only pollinator.

CLEARED FOR LANDING

Markings in the center of dwarf iris petals lead bees and other pollinators to the flowers' nectar. Over time, many plants and their pollinators have adapted to each other's ways.

34

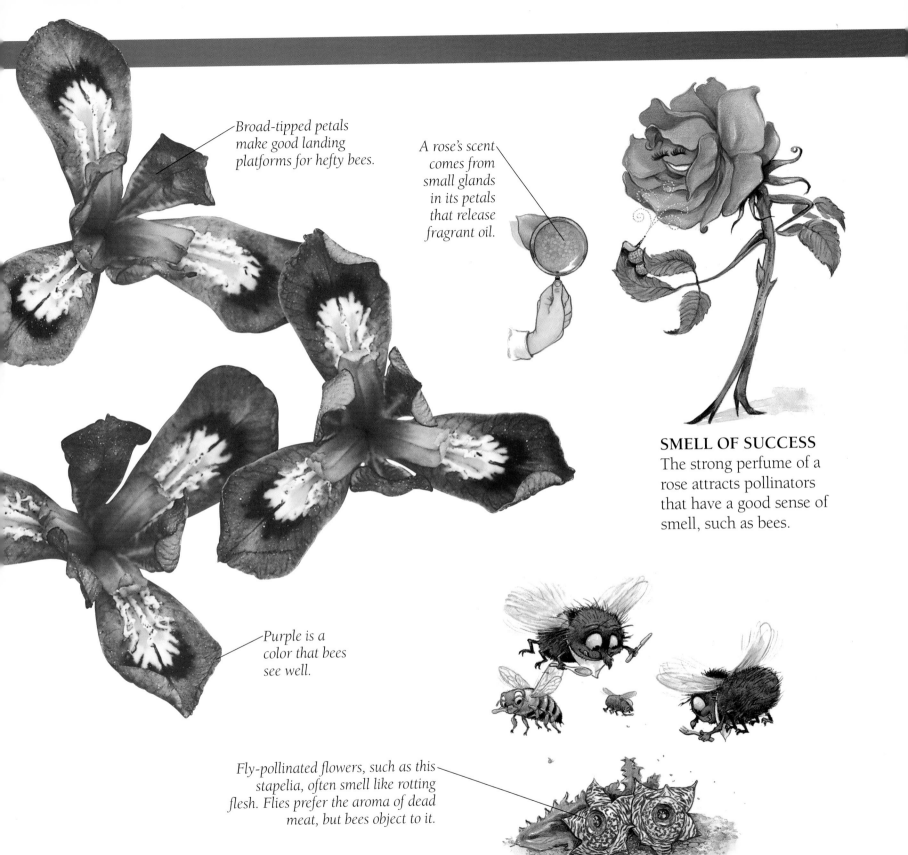

Broad-tipped petals make good landing platforms for hefty bees.

A rose's scent comes from small glands in its petals that release fragrant oil.

SMELL OF SUCCESS

The strong perfume of a rose attracts pollinators that have a good sense of smell, such as bees.

Purple is a color that bees see well.

Fly-pollinated flowers, such as this stapelia, often smell like rotting flesh. Flies prefer the aroma of dead meat, but bees object to it.

Pollen Partners

Insects are the chief pollinators of flowering plants, with birds coming in second. Even mammals get into the act. They, too, go after nutritious nectar and pollen. Animals, including insects, may eat as much as three-fourths of a plant's pollen, but they still carry enough away on their snouts, feet, or other body parts to transfer the dust to the next flower they encounter.

POLLEN POSSUM
A honey possum, a tiny relative of the kangaroo, sips nectar from a banksia plant in Australia. A long, brushy tongue helps the honey possum mop up the sweet liquid.

Bats feed at night. Light-colored flowers with strong scents attract these flying mammals.

BAT TREAT
Its head already dusted with pollen, a long-nosed bat lashes out toward supper—possibly a cactus flower.

Even with its extra-long tongue, this bat gets pollen on its head when it dines at a flower.

FLAX FRIEND

A New Zealand gecko, a kind of lizard, tastes the nectar of a flax plant at night. The "bib" of pollen the gecko collects will rub off as it eats its next meal.

The long, pollen-tipped anthers of the flax plant "paint" the pollen on the gecko's body.

IN-FLIGHT MEAL

A ruby-throated hummingbird probes for nectar in a feathery celosia. Since hummingbirds hover while they feed, the flowers they prefer don't need wide petals that can serve as landing platforms.

6 A Seed Is Borne

After pollination and fertilization, a flower produces seeds. These range in size. Begonia seeds are the size of fine grains of sand, while the largest coconut has a seed that weighs 40 pounds. Seeds usually travel some distance to find space to grow. They use many forms of transportation. Some seeds, wearing wings or parachutes, fly or drift to their new locations. Others, like that of the coconut, ride waves to distant shores.

TIME TRAVELER
Palm trees growing on tropical shores often send their fruit—coconuts—on incredible journeys. A coconut may float hundreds of miles before it lands and the seed inside sprouts.

Wind can carry the seeds for miles.

BUCKEYE BLAST
The smooth, ripe pod of the red buckeye tree is a fruit that splits, scattering its shiny brown seeds.

UP, UP, AND AWAY
A fluffy, fully seeded dandelion is a ready target for the wind—or a kid at play. Each small seed comes loose from the plant attached to its own wispy parachute.

Before it ripened, this buckeye pod was covered with prickly spines.

38

Maple wings start out droopy, but spread wide as the seeds ripen.

AIR FREIGHT

Seeds on a Norway maple develop in pairs. Each pair comes supplied with stiff wings that act like helicopter rotors when the seeds are blown off the tree.

SKY DIVERS

A milkweed seed, close up, shows the fine fluff that forms its parachute. The seeds grow in sturdy pods that split open when the seed is ready to travel.

When ripe, the seedpods of the Scotch broom snap open, shooting tiny seeds in all directions.

Hitching a Ride

Air and water don't get all seeds where they need to go. Many seeds travel by other methods, using all kinds of animals as transportation. Seeds may hitch a ride somewhere on the outside of an animal. But a lot of seeds travel inside seed-eating animals. The seeds go where the animal goes and are distributed in its droppings.

MONSTER MOVER ▶
A grizzly bear in Alaska munches blades of grass. Any seeds in the grass will travel inside the bear and may be deposited in another part of its territory.

STOP, DROP, AND GROW
Perching birds take a break—and contribute to the future of plants with their droppings.

Bohemian waxwing

FUR BURR
A burr, a seedpod covered with spines, travels in the tangles of a shaggy dog's coat. The burr may fall off or may come loose when the dog scratches itself.

HOP ON SOCKS
Our socks sometimes act in the same way as an animal's fur, picking up prickly burrs. These may end up in the wash before they have a chance to drop off. The ring-shaped pods of the devil's claw may become an ankle bracelet for a cow. Seeds fall out as the cow roams.

40

A Plant Grows Up

Often, seeds don't germinate, or sprout, as soon as they hit the ground. Seeds that ripen close to winter usually wait until the next spring before sprouting. Some seeds may lie on or in the soil for years, waiting for the right combination of water, light, and warmth to get them started.

THE FIRE OF LIFE

Sometimes it takes fire to make a seed sprout or a plant grow. New shoots of grass trees in western Australia grow only after they have been exposed to fire. Fire also opens the tough seedpods of banksia and other plants and releases the seeds.

SEEK THE LIGHT

Newly sprouted plants, called seedlings, bend toward an indoor light. They need the light for growth and for photosynthesis.

FROM SEED TO SEEDLING

Under the ground, a seed sends down a root. Along with the embryo, or tiny plant, inside it, the seed contains food for early growth. As the root branches out, the seed pops above ground on its stem. Two leaves appear, called seed leaves, that look unlike those that will grow later. Growth continues above and below the ground. True leaves form as the stem continues upward, and the seed leaves shrivel. Roots branch, and branch again.

NOT-YET-MIGHTY OAK

This oak seedling sprouted from an acorn— the fruit of an oak tree. Each acorn actually contains several seeds. Squirrels "plant" oaks when they bury acorns.

The seed of this pine seedling formed inside a female pine cone.

PINE PUSH-UP

A pine seedling pushes upward, its first leaves unfolding at the top of its stem. Trees need space and plenty of light to continue to grow. Seedlings that start too close to the parent tree usually don't survive.

43

All Grown Up

One in a million acorns grows to become a mature oak tree. An acorn is a tempting treat to squirrels and other animals. Even if the oak reaches sapling stage as a young tree, it still attracts animals such as deer that favor its tender shoots. Only when it becomes established, after about 20 years, does an oak's future look more secure. It still provides food for animals, but is strong enough to survive their nibbling.

LOOKIN' GOOD
A pine sapling grows in a forest clearing. The tree that fell has probably given the pine a chance for a good start. Bushy and bright green, it seems to be getting enough light as well as nourishment from the soil.

A LIFE STORY
An oak seedling is like a human infant. The fragile sprout needs just the right conditions to grow properly. As a sapling, the oak is like a teenager. It uses a lot of energy to grow taller, but still has a long way to go. Like a grown-up, a mature oak tree can help other organisms. It can take up to 200 years for an oak to reach full maturity.

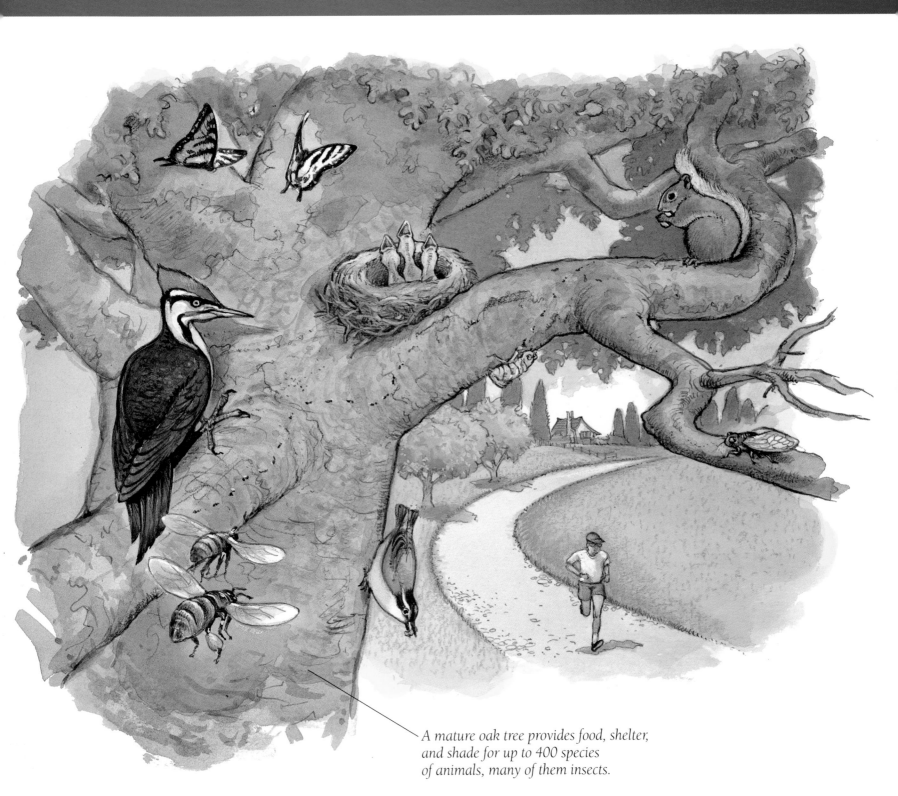

A mature oak tree provides food, shelter, and shade for up to 400 species of animals, many of them insects.

8

Fancy Feast

Some plants "hunt" for food because they need insect meals to round out their diets. Insectivorous (in-seck-TIV-eh-ruhs), or insect-eating, plants usually live in bogs and swamps where the soil is low in nutrients. Since they can't chase down prey, these insectivorous plants have developed ways of trapping insects that come near.

Once an insect is trapped in the sticky stalks of a sundew, the leaves bend around to digest it.

DEW AND DIE
Like dewdrops sparkling in the sun, the sundew's secretions, or liquids its cells make, attract insects. The secretions work like flypaper. An insect landing on a glistening stalk sticks tight. The insect is dissolved by other secretions and absorbed into the sundew.

DEADLY DRINK
Shaped like a cup with a large lid, the northern pitcher plant lures insects with nectar. Insects slide down the slippery walls of the cup and drown in rainwater collected at the bottom.

A hollow leaf forms the cup of a pitcher plant.

FLY JUICE
This pitcher plant's lid and rim are cut away to show the drowning pool inside. Trapped insects float in a special liquid that dissolves their bodies so the plant can absorb nutrients in liquid form.

DEATH TRAP

The Venus's-flytrap, native to North and South Carolina, catches insects with its hinged leaves rimmed with bristles. Each plant contains a number of the specialized leaves known as traps. Flytraps also photosynthesize and will not trap insects if there are enough minerals in the soil.

FLIES, BEWARE!

Each side of a trap contains several hairs that detect motion. When an insect touches the trigger hairs more than once within a short time, the leaf clamps shut. Tiny insects may escape the prison of bristles, but larger ones, such as flies, usually become permanent captives.

People should never feed flytraps hamburger meat. It can kill the plants.

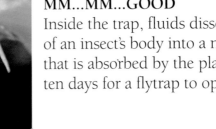

MM...MM...GOOD

Inside the trap, fluids dissolve the soft parts of an insect's body into a nourishing liquid that is absorbed by the plant. It takes up to ten days for a flytrap to open after a meal.

47

⬤9 Communities

People, like plants, often live in groups. But while people can choose where they want to live, plants cannot. Over millions of years, plants have adapted to the earth's different habitats. Plants that grow together naturally in a certain kind of habitat, such as a desert, form a plant community.

DOWN BY THE SEA

Plants that inhabit the seaside must be strong enough to stand up to the awesome power of sea, sun, and wind. They must also be able to thrive in salty sand. Beach grass is one plant that meets the challenge. It anchors itself with roots, then sends out underground stems from which new plants sprout.

Grass plants help preserve a dune by gripping the sand and keeping it from blowing away.

INTO THE WOODS

In a woodland, plants grow at different levels. The tallest trees provide the leafy roof of the forest, called a canopy. Shorter trees make up the understory. Below them live shrubs, or bushes. Plants such as ferns come next. Mosses sprout at the lowest level, the forest floor.

DESERT DRAMA
Desert plants, such as these inhabitants of Utah, are true survivors. They stand up to intense sun and heat and very little rainfall. Most desert plants store water in leaves, stems, or roots.

WET AND WILD
Wetland plants grow in, on, and near water. They may grow in water that is fresh, salty, or a combination of both. Their stems and leaves often have air spaces inside that help them float.

49

10 Plants in Our Lives

Plants are necessary for most life on earth. Nearly all forms of life rely in some way on the photosynthesis that takes place in the leaves of plants. Plants provide oxygen and food for animals—and the animals that eat other animals. Plants offer people food, clothing, and shelter. They are also important in the development of medicines.

cocoa tree

LEND AN EAR

When we brush an ear of corn with butter and begin to munch, we are eating the seeds of the corn plant. The white, starchy part inside every kernel is the food the corn seed contains to nourish a sprouting seedling.

The Madagascar periwinkle plant is often made into a medicine that helps fight cancer.

Oranges supply vitamin C that helps keep us healthy.

LEAF FOR RELIEF

Inside the broad leaf of the aloe (AH-low) plant is a kind of gel that soothes dry skin and mild burns. Aloes came originally from the West Indies.

cotton plant

Aloes store moisture in their thick leaves.

SIZING UP SISAL
Spiky leaves up to ten feet tall grow on the barrel-shaped stem of the sisal hemp plant. Sisal leaves are used to make rope.

Braided sisal fibers make strong ropes, nets, hammocks, and twine.

SPICE OF LIFE
Baskets of spices decorate an outdoor market in France. The seeds, flowers, berries, and leaves of many plants add color and flavor to foods in kitchens all over the world.

◄ PLENTIFUL PLANT PRODUCTS
From cotton for clothing to cocoa for hot chocolate, plant products improve our lives.

51

How Does Your Garden Grow?

Many of us live in houses that were built on land cleared of trees and other plants. People enjoy the beauty of plants, however, so they grow trees, bushes, or flowers around the buildings they live in. Gardeners have many choices for the kinds of plants they can use to make their homes and yards pretty. Plants beautify our surroundings throughout the world—and they make life on earth possible.

While they add beauty to the world, plants offer animals places to hide and to feed.

GLORIOUS GARDEN
People like plants—and so do other animals. This family used a variety of plants, including those that live in water, to make their yard a friendly place for many different animals.

BOX OF BLOOMS
Multicolored petunias overflow a window box on this Vermont house. Home gardeners can start their flowers from seeds or from young plants.

Name That Plant

Plants, like most living things, have two kinds of names. One is the Latin name scientists give to describe a plant's features and relationship to other plants. The other is the common name, a kind of nickname for the plant. Often, both the scientific name and the common name are based on the plant's looks. Before you read about them, can you guess the common names of these plants?

Bleeding heart flowers hang from leafless stalks.

The blooms of the bleeding heart grow in pairs.

LIKE A ROLLING...
Though they're smooth as pebbles on the bottom of a stream, these plants grow in Africa's Namib Desert. Called living stones, they have fleshy tissue that holds moisture. They bear a single white flower.

ACHY BREAKY…

These flowers start out as long ovals dangling from a stem. As they grow, they puff into the shape that inspired the plant's name—bleeding heart.

At the end of the growing season, the seedpods of this garden plant rub off easily, revealing silvery disks slightly larger than a quarter that gave the plant its common name—money plant.

WHAT'S FOR BREAKFAST?

Two eggs— scrambled, please— would go well with the fruit of this African plant. It got its name—sausage tree—from the shape of its fruit.

55

Did You Know...

1 **THAT** the daisy-like compass plant lines itself up with the path of the sun? About half the plant will point east, while the other half will point west. This plant once grew in abundance across the North American plains, helping the pioneers find their way across the continent.

2 **THAT** plants exposed to certain kinds of music may actually grow taller and stronger than plants that don't "listen" to music? Not any kind of music will do, though. Plants seem to prefer the more soothing strains of classical music than the pounding beat of heavy rock.

3 **THAT** the baobab (BOW-bob) tree of Africa can store up to 25,000 gallons of water in its spongy trunk and lower branches? The stored water helps this deciduous tree survive through a long dry season.

4 **THAT** some flowers lead an insect through a kind of maze to reach their pollen? The route is one-way, and the insect is sure to carry some pollen away as it heads for freedom.

POLLEN

5 **THAT** when a saguaro cactus ages and dies, its green outer "skin" and spines wear away to reveal a kind of skeleton inside? The cactus skeleton is not made of bone, but of woody ribs that supported the tall, heavy plant while it was alive.

6 **THAT** the giant Amazon water lily grows leaves that are up to six feet across? They float like huge rafts on the surface of still water, held up by stems up to 35 feet long. The largest leaves can support up to 160 pounds, about the weight of a young tapir, an animal related to horses and rhinos.

Glossary

ANTHER Part of the stamen that makes and stores pollen.

CELL The smallest unit of a living thing that can function independently.

CHLOROPHYLL Particles in the leaves of green plants that absorb energy from sunlight and start the process of photosynthesis.

DECIDUOUS Trees that shed all their leaves once a year.

EVERGREEN Trees that bear leaves all year long, shedding a small number of leaves continuously.

FERTILIZATION The union of a male pollen grain and a female egg cell in a cone or flower that leads to the production of seeds.

FLOWER The part of a flowering plant that contains all the structures needed for reproduction.

GERMINATION The sprouting of a seed that begins a plant's growth.

GLUCOSE A sugary food made by a plant through photosynthesis.

LEAF A part of the plant attached to a stem in which photosynthesis occurs.

NECTAR A sweet liquid made in a flower that attracts insects and other animals that spread the flower's pollen.

OVARY The base of the pistil containing the egg. After the egg is fertilized, the ovary develops into a fruit that contains seeds.

PHOTOSYNTHESIS The process in which the leaves of a plant use sunlight, air, and water to manufacture food for the plant.

PISTIL The female part of a flower containing the stigma, style, and ovary.

POLLEN Tiny spores produced by male cones and also by the anthers of flowering plants.

POLLINATION The process in which pollen is transferred from one flower to another of the same species to fertilize it.

ROOT The part of the plant that usually grows underground and anchors it, absorbs water and nutrients, and sometimes stores food for the plant.

SEED The fertilized structure of a cone-bearing or flowering plant that can produce a new plant.

SPORES Cells produced by plants such as ferns that lead to the formation of new plants. Pollen is also a kind of spore.

STAMEN The male part of a flowering plant formed of the anther and the filament, the stalk that supports it.

STEM The usually upright, aboveground part of a plant that develops shoots and leaves.

STIGMA A female part of a flower plant that receives pollen during pollination.

STYLE The connecting stalk between the stigma and the ovary of a flowering plant.

Index

Credits

pansy

Published by
The National Geographic Society
Reg Murphy, *President
and Chief Executive Officer*
Gilbert M. Grosvenor,
Chairman of the Board
Nina D. Hoffman,
Senior Vice President
William R. Gray, *Vice President and Director, Book Division*

Staff for this Book
Barbara Lalicki, *Director of Children's Publishing*
Barbara Brownell, *Senior Editor and Project Manager*
Marianne R. Koszorus, *Senior Art Director and Project Manager*
Toni Eugene, *Editor*
Alexandra Littlehales, *Art Director*
Susan V. Kelly, *Illustrations Editor*
Joyce B. Marshall, *Researcher*
Jennifer Emmett, *Assistant Editor*
Meredith Wilcox, *Illustrations Assistant*
Elisabeth MacRae-Bobynskyj, *Indexer*
Mark A. Caraluzzi, *Marketing Manager*
Vincent P. Ryan, *Manufacturing Manager*
Lewis R. Bassford, *Production Project Manager*

Acknowledgments

We are grateful for the assistance of Holly H. Shimizu, Managing Director, Lewis Ginter Botanical Garden, *Scientific Consultant*. We also thank John Agnone and Rebecca Lescaze, National Geographic Book Division, for their guidance and suggestions.

Illustrations Credits

COVER Stephen G. St. John/NGS Image Collection
Interior Photographs from the Earth Scenes Division of Animals Animals Enterprises.
Front Matter: 1 F. Prenzel. 2-3 George F. Godfrey. 4 (top to bottom), Scott W. Smith; E.R. Degginger; Richard Shiell; John Gerlach. 5 (top to bottom), Patti Murray; Rich Reid; Art Phaneuf. 6-7 (art), Warren Cutler. 8 (art), Warren Cutler. 9 (art), Robert Cremins. 9 Breck P. Kent. 10 (left to right), Bates Littlehales; Donald Specker; Scott W. Smith. 11 (art), Warren Cutler. 12 (art), Warren Cutler. 12 Robert Maier. 13 (left upper), Patti Murray; (right upper), Robert Maier; (lower), C.C. Lockwood. 14 (art), Robert Cremins. 14 John Gerlach. 15 (art), Robert Cremins. 15 Don Skillman.
Once a Plant: 16 (art), Robert Cremins. 16 John Eastcott/Yva Momatiuk. 17 (art), Warren Cutler. 17 Doug Allan. 18 (art), Robert Cremins. 18 E.R. Degginger. 19 Robert Maier.
First on Land: 20 (left to right), Robert Maier; Michael P. Gadomski; Photography by Thane. 21 (art), Robert Cremins.
Plants Take Hold: 22 (art), Warren Cutler. 22 (both left), G.I. Bernard; (right) Nigel Smith. 23 (art), Warren Cutler. 23 Richard Kolar. 24 (art), Warren Cutler. 24 G.I. Bernard. 25 (left), Stan Osolinsky; (right) Richard Shiell. 26 (art), Robert Cremins. 26 Bates Littlehales. 27 (art), Robert Cremins. 27 (left to right), Robert A. Lubeck; G.I. Bernard; Tom Edwards, Phil Degginger.
Conifers and Cousins: 28 (art), Warren Cutler. 28 David J. Boyle. 29 Richard Shiell.
Flowering Plants: 30 (art), Robert Cremins. 31 John A. Anderson. 32 (art), Robert Cremins. 32 (left), Stephen Dalton; (right), Bill Beatty. 33 (art), Warren Cutler. 33 Stephen Dalton. 34 (art), Warren Cutler. 34 Fritz Prenzel.34-35 John Gerlach. 35 (art), Robert Cremins. 36 (art), Warren Cutler. 36 (left), OSF; (right), Babs & Bert Wells. 37 (art) Warren Cutler. 37 Marcia W. Griffen.
A Seed Is Borne: 38 (art), Robert Cremins. 38 (upper), C.C. Lockwood; (lower), Patti Murray. 39 (art), Robert Cremins. 39 (upper), Patti Murray; (lower), Bill Beatty. 40 (art, upper), Warren Cutler; (lower, both), Robert Cremins. 40 Breck P. Kent. 41 Lynn M. Stone.
A Plant Grows Up: 42 (art), Warren Cutler. 42 E.R. Degginger. 43 (art), Robert Cremins. 43 (left), Robert Maier; (right), Jack Wilburn. 44 (art, both), Robert Cremins. 44 David J. Boyle. 45 (art), Robert Cremins.
Fancy Feast: 46 (art), Warren Cutler. 46 (left), Patti Murray; (right), Donald Specker. 47 (art), Robert Cremins. 47 (top to bottom), Patti Murray; Breck P. Kent; Breck P. Kent.
Communities: 48 (art), Warren Cutler. 48 Bates Littlehales. 49 (left), Rich Reid; (right), Michael P. Gadomski.
Plants in Our Lives: 50 (art), Warren Cutler. 50 (upper), Michael P. Gadomski; (lower), Fred Whitehead. 51 (art), Robert Cremins. 51 (upper), Hans and Judy Beste; (lower), Robert Maier. 52 John L. Pontier. 52-53 Warren Cutler. 54 Breck P. Kent. 55 (art), Robert Cremins. 55 (upper), Art Phaneuf; (lower), Zig Leszczynski.
Back Matter: 56 (art, both), Robert Cremins; 56 Ted Levin. 57 (upper art), Warren Cutler. 57 (lower art), Robert Cremins. 57 Ted Levin. 60 Patti Murray.

COVER: Honeybees gather pollen and nectar from a sunflower; seeds have begun to form in the center of the flower.

Composition for this book by the National Geographic Society Book Division. Printed and bound by R.R. Donnelley & Sons Company, Willard, Ohio. Color separations by Quad Graphics, Martinsburg, West Virginia. Case cover printed by Inland Press, Menomonee Falls, Wisconsin.

Library of Congress CIP Data
Howell, Catherine Herbert.
    Plants / by Catherine Herbert Howell.
        p.   cm — (National Geographic nature library)
    Includes index.
    Summary: Examines characteristics of plants, their varying habitats, different species, and the process of photosynthesis.
    ISBN 0-7922-7045-2
    1. Plants—Juvenile literature. [1. Plants.]   I. National Geographic Society (U.S.)
II. Title III. Series.
QK49.H68   1997
580—dc21
                                              97-28649
                                                      CIP
                                                         AC